DATE DUE

~~MR 24 0~~			
~~MY 21 0~~			
~~JE 8 08~~			

DEMCO 38-296

CAMP NOTES
AND OTHER POEMS

MITSUYE YAMADA

KITCHEN TABLE: Women of Color Press

My affectionate thanks to Alta and Angel who have coaxed *Camp Notes* out of mothballs.

Camp Notes and Other Poems was originally published by Shameless Hussy Press in 1976.

Cover design by Smith and Jones Communications, Troy, NY.
Text design by The Type Set, New York, NY.
Illustrations by Jeni Yamada.
Calligraphy by Yoshikazu Yamada.
Typesetting by The Type Set.

Printed on acid-free paper by Patterson Printing, Benton Harbor, MI.

Second Edition. First Printing.

ISBN 0-913175-23-4 paper.
ISBN 0-913175-24-2 cloth.

For my mother, Hide.
In memory of my father, Jack.
And for Yosh and our children
Jeni, Phil, Steve, Kai, Heidi
and all sansei and yonsei
who keep us alive.

TABLE OF CONTENTS

III OTHER POEMS

I. MY ISSEI PARENTS
TWICE PIONEERS
NOW I HEAR THEM

母が今言ふ十事
其内に分つて来る、

WHAT YOUR MOTHER TELLS YOU

haha ga ima yu-koto
sono uchi ni
wakatte kuru

What your mother tells you now
in time
you will come to know.

☐

GREAT GRANDMA

great
grandmama's savings
in boxed dividers:
colored stones
yellowed yarns
pine cones
fabric scraps
brown bags pressed
dried seaweeds
parched persimmons
bitter melon seeds
powdery green tea
leaves

life's allotment
she'd say
when used up
time to die

□

MARRIAGE WAS A FOREIGN COUNTRY

I come to be here
because
they say I must
follow my husband

so I come.

My grandmother cried:
you are not cripple
why
to America?

When we land the boat full
of new brides
lean over railing
with wrinkled glossy pictures
they hold inside hand
like this
so excited
down there a dock full of men
they do same thing
hold pictures
look up and down
like this
they find faces to
match pictures.

Your father I see him on the dock
he come to Japan to marry
and leave me
I was not a picture bride
I only was afraid.

☐

HOMECOMING

from Tillie Olsen

I widow
redo my life
scratch out lies
lie buried inside
the house all the time
sorrows my nights
cries still survive.

You child
chide me too
often look cross
eye not see me cry
alone widow after thirty-five
years have final right to live.

My first born your brother
all the time in my arms
cry his scrotum swell
screech in my ears
I cry alone
no sleep for me.

My second born
a son too
sickly brothers
born so close
together we cry
there was no one
else.

I was sick with you
soon to come
Papa say go home
to your mother in Japan
you born there
but my boys need me at home

in America
I must leave you there
with wet nurse
we send for you
later nothing else to do.

You only a girl
do not know what I suffer
you blame me too
much sickness in you
when you come home to us
we take you to hospital
at home I have two sons
your father and no help
no night nurse I
stay up with you
whine after me
when I leave.

Loving you
could not know
what pains to live
without love
my friend kill
herself hang
her family with eight children
don't know
how she could
do it for good reason
I think of her often
bring me comfort.

So little you run
home everyday after school
because there you hope
to find Mama
alive.

□

A BEDTIME STORY

Once upon a time,
an old Japanese legend
goes as told
by Papa,
an old woman traveled through
many small villages
seeking refuge
for the night.
Each door opened
a sliver
in answer to her knock
then closed.
Unable to walk
any further
she wearily climbed a hill
found a clearing
and there lay down to rest
a few moments to catch
her breath.

The village town below
lay asleep except
for a few starlike lights.
Suddenly the clouds opened
and a full moon came into view
over the town.

The old woman sat up
turned toward
the village town

and in supplication
called out
Thank you people
of the village,
if it had not been for your
kindness
in refusing me a bed
for the night
these humble eyes would never
have seen this
memorable sight.

Papa paused, I waited.
In the comfort of our
hilltop home in Seattle
overlooking the valley,
I shouted
"That's the *end?*"

☐

遠慮

ENRYO

Enryo is a Japanese word
which sounds like
in leo.
What does being in a lion
have to do with humility
I asked Papa
who said
could be
since lions are
by tradition
regally proud
ENRYO is pride
in disguise.

Even so
it is holding back
saying no
thank you
saying no
trouble at all.

☐

DIALOGUE

I said

Don't
after twenty years
you know
she's leaving
you
must listen to
her
stop
and listen.

He said

But I did
I called her in here
I asked
her
I hear
you have something
on your mind
WHAT
but she stood right
there
dumb
looking out
the window.

□

II. CAMP NOTES

EVACUATION

As we boarded the bus
bags on both sides
(I had never packed
two bags before
on a vacation
lasting forever)
the *Seattle Times*
photographer said
Smile!
so obediently I smiled
and the caption the next day
read:

Note smiling faces
a lesson to Tokyo.

□

ON THE BUS

Who goes?
Not the leaders of the people
combed out and left
with the FBI.
Our father
stayed behind
triple locks.
What was the charge?
Possible espionage or
impossible espionage.
I forgot which.

Only those who remained
free in prisons
stayed behind.

The rest of us went to
Camp Harmony
where the first baby
was christened

Melody.

☐

HARMONY AT THE FAIR GROUNDS

Why is the soldier boy in a cage
like that?
In the freedom of the child's
universe
the uniformed guard
stood trapped in his outside cage.
We walked away from the gate and
grated guard
on sawdusted grounds
where millions trod once
to view prize cows
at the Puyallup Fair.

They gave us straws to sleep on
encased in muslin ticks.
Some of us were stalled under grandstand
seats
the egg with
parallel lines.

Lines formed for food
lines for showers
lines for the john
lines for shots.

☐

CURFEW

In our area
was a block head
who told us
what's what
in a warden's helmet.

Turn off your lights
it's curfew time!

I was reading
with a flashlight
under my blanket
but the barracks boards
in the hot sun
had shrunk slyly
telling
bars of light

Off with your lights.

There must be no light.

☐

MINIDOKA, IDAHO

In Minidoka
I ordered a pair of white
majorette boots
with tassels from
Montgomery Ward
and swaggered in
ankle deep dust.

I heard
bullsnakes were sprinkled
along the edges
to rid us of dread
rattlers.
A few of their orphans
hatched and escaped behind
barbed wires
befriended by boys
with mayonnaise jars.

Let them go I said to Joe
they will poison us.
But they are lost, and see? Blind
said Joe.
We rescued them
from the bullies.

☐

BLOCK 4 BARRACK 4 "APT" C

The barbed fence
protected us
from wildly twisted
sagebrush.
Some were taken
by old men with gnarled
hands.
These sinewed branches
were rubbed and polished
shiny with sweat and body oil.

They creeped on
under and around our coffee table
with apple crate stands.

Lives spilled over us
through plaster walls
came mixed voices.
Bared too
a pregnant wife
while her man played *go*
all day
she sobbed alone
and a barracksful
of ears shed tears.

☐

DESERT STORM

Near the mess hall
along the latrines
by the laundry
between the rows of
black tar papered barracks
the block captain galloped by.
Take cover everyone he said
here comes a twister.

Hundreds of windows
slammed shut.
Five pairs of hands
in our room
with mess hall
butter knives
stuffed
newspapers and rags
between the cracks.
But the Idaho dust
persistent and seeping
found us crouched
under the covers.

This was not
im
prison
ment.
This was
re
location.

□

IN THE OUTHOUSE

Our collective wastebin
where the air sticks
in my craw
burns my eyes
I have this place to hide
the excreta and
the blood which
do not flush down
nor seep away.

They pile up
fill the earth.

I am drowning.

□

INSIDE NEWS

A small group
huddles around a contraband
radio
What?
We
are losing the war?
Who is we?
We are we the enemy
the enemy is the enemy.

Static sounds and we
cannot hear.
The enemy is confused
the enemy is determined
and winning.

Mess hall gossips
have it that
the parents
with samurai morals
are now the children.

□

THE WATCHTOWER

The watchtower
with one uniformed
guard
in solitary
confined in the middle
of his land.

I walked towards the hospital
for the midnight shift.
From the rec hall the long body
of the centipede
with barracks for legs
came the sound of a
live band playing
Maria Elena
You're the answer to my dreams.
Tired teenagers
leaning on each other
swayed without struggle.

This is what we did with our days.
We loved and we lived
just like people.

☐

RECRUITING TEAM

Returning from the hospital
on duty all night
I stopped to watch a curious crowd
around two Army uniforms
old men shouting from their fringes
Baka ya ro nani yutto ru ka
Dumbbells! We don't believe you!
Inside circle listening
outside circle shouting
Bakani suruna
Don't make fools of us.
A bent spoon hit me
on the head.
I swung around and saw
I saw hundreds of fixed eyes
listening and not listening
to voices
beating
signals in the desert.

I put my hands over
my ears and
ran
but one
lone
voice
pursued me:

Why should I volunteer!
I'm an American
I have a right to be
drafted.

☐

P.O.W.

I sit
inside these fences
and forget
all my miseries
were left outside.

☐

My daily routine
of going to the mess hall
has nothing to do with
my appetite.

☐

— Jakki

Jakki was the penname of my father, Jack Yasutake,
formerly an interpreter for the Immigration Service, who
was interned by the FBI during the years 1941-1944.
These are translations of two of his senryu poems.

SEARCH AND RESCUE

We joined the party
for the feel of freedom.
What are we looking for
among gnarled knuckles
in sagebrush forest?

>An old man
>out of his head
>wandered off they said.
>We're scouts
>to help him across the gate.

In a straight line
we inched over
his twisted trail.
Is he bio
degradable
half buried in desert dust?

>He must be degraved,
>pulled up, potted, niched
>up against the stone wall.

>Enshrined.

☐

THE TRICK WAS

The trick was
keep the body busy
be a teacher
be a nurse
be a typist
read some write some
poems
write Papa in prison
write to schools
(one hundred thirty-three colleges
in the whole United States in the back
of my Webster's dictionary
answered: no admittance
THEY were afraid of ME)

But the mind was not fooled.

☐

SOME PEOPLE WALKED THROUGH

Some people walked through
and out the back of my mind.

I'll bet you a home-made apple pie
you'll never get out of here in
a hundred years.
    That's impossible.
    Where in the world would you
    get apples?
Okay then I'll bet you
a million dollars.

What a pretty garden you made, Obasan.
    No, this is not much.
    The one I had in Seattle had
    many beautiful flowers.
Too bad we are not in Seattle.
    Sore wa shikata ga ari masen ne?
    That can't be helped can it?

What's your name?
    Bo ya
Whose boy are you?
    Nobody's
(Pinned on his back was a sign:
Please do not feed me.)

    □

MESS HALL DISCIPLINE

The mother drew my eyes
to her smiling mouth
but still I saw her
pinch her daughter who let drop
the handful of mushy beans
shrieked a soundless cry
and abundant tears.

☐

THE QUESTION OF LOYALTY

I met the deadline
for alien registration
once before
was numbered fingerprinted
and ordered not to travel
without permit.

But alien still they said I must
foreswear allegiance to the emperor.
For me that was easy
I didn't even know him
but my mother who did cried out
    If I sign this
    What will I be?
    I am doubly loyal
    to my American children
    also to my own people.
    How can double mean nothing?
    I wish no one to lose this war.
    Everyone does.

I was poor
at math.
I signed
my only ticket out.

☐

THE NIGHT BEFORE GOOD-BYE

Mama is mending
my underwear
while my brothers sleep.
Her husband taken away by the FBI
one son lured away by the Army
now another son and daughter
lusting for the free world outside.
She must let go.
The war goes on.
She will take one still small son
and join Papa in internment
to make a family.
Still sewing
squinting in the dim light
in room C barrack 4 block 4
she whispers
Remember
keep your underwear
in good repair
in case of accident
don't bring shame
on us.

☐

THIRTY YEARS UNDER

I had packed up
my wounds in a cast
iron box
sealed it
labeled it
do not open. . .
ever. . .

and traveled blind
for thirty years

until one day I heard
a black man with huge bulbous eyes
say
there is nothing more
humiliating
more than beatings
more than curses
than being spat on

like a dog.

☐

CINCINNATI

Freedom at last
in this town aimless
I walked against the rush
hour traffic
My first day
in a real city
where

no one knew me.

No one except one
hissing voice that said
dirty jap
warm spittle on my right cheek.
I turned and faced
the shop window
and my spittled face
spilled onto a hill
of books.
Words on display.

In Government Square
people criss-crossed
the street
like the spokes of
a giant wheel.

I lifted my right hand
but it would not obey me.

My other hand fumbled
for a hankie.

My tears would not
wash it. They stopped
and parted.
My hankie brushed
the forked
tears and spittle
together.
I edged toward the curb
loosened my fisthold
and the bleached laced
mother-ironed hankie blossomed in
the gutter atop teeth marked
gum wads and heeled candy wrappers.

Everyone knew me.

☐

III. OTHER POEMS

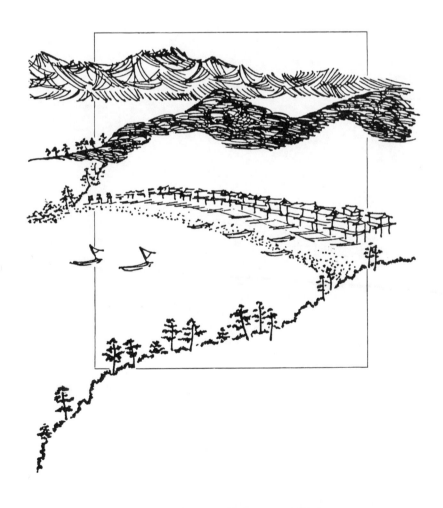

FREEDOM IN MANHATTAN

We were three girls
minding our distance
two thousand miles from home
crouched in darkness behind
the covered bathtub
in the kitchen.
To some boys
we weren't home
in this cold water flat
one jump from the East River.

Voices and hard knuckles
banged away on our door
Let us in, Harry sent us.

Lock up boys for
knocking up your door?
roared the sergeant behind
his desk, Come back,
come back when ya got
real troubles.
Our hands clutched
the playpen railing
He licked the point of his
pencil and waved it
back and forth over our souls.

The next day
hard fists
knocked on, unhinged
and battered
our defenses.

We were three big girls
in red shoelaces
winding down the
squadcar window
looking for
Mr. Knuckles.

They drove us once
around the block then back to
one jump from the East River.
Look girls, don't make trouble.
Move out, move out, they said.
But the rent's cheap, we said.
Virgins are cheaper, they said.

☐

LOOKING OUT

It must be odd
to be a minority
he was saying.
I looked around
and didn't see any.
So I said
Yeah
it must be.

☐

TO THE LADY

The one in San Francisco who asked
Why did the Japanese Americans let
the government put them in
those camps without protest?

Come to think of it I

  should've run off to Canada
  should've hijacked a plane to Algeria
  should've pulled myself up from my
  bra straps
  and kicked'm in the groin
  should've bombed a bank
  should've tried self-immolation
  should've holed myself up in a
  woodframe house
  and let you watch me
  burn up on the six o'clock news
  should've run howling down the street
  naked and assaulted you at breakfast
  by AP wirephoto
  should've screamed bloody murder
  like Kitty Genovese

Then

YOU would've

    come to my aid in shining armor
    laid yourself across the railroad track
    marched on Washington
    tattooed a Star of David on your arm
    written six million enraged
    letters to Congress

But we didn't draw the line
anywhere
law and order Executive Order 9066
social order moral order internal order

YOU let'm
I let'm
All are punished.

□

HERE

I was always
a starting person
like sprouts and shoots
or a part person
like slices and slivers
which is why
neighbor boys called out
MIT SUEY CHOP SUEY

☐

THERE

Once when I went back
to where I came from
I was sent to school
in clothes "Made in Japan"
and small children along
the riverbank stopped jumping
rope and sing-sang:

America no ojo-o san
doko ni iku-u
America no ojo-o san
doko ni iku-u

Girl from America
where are you going?
Girl from America
where are you going?

□

THE SPEECH

Zambia stood before the Council of Churches
a prepared text held upright
under one corner of the dashiki
covering his black naked body.
The delegates in silent hundreds
stood openly
ready and willing for the roar
to tear their flesh.

"We..."
Then for five full minutes,
Zambia, 50, wept.

☐

THE FOUNDATION

This could be the land
where everything grows.
Bulldozers had sifted up
large pieces of parched woods and
worthless rocks.
Bilateral buildings
to be are not yet.

Meanwhile on this dust
I counted seven shapes
of sturdy greys and greens
some small and slender
vertical parallels.
No one planted them here with squared T's.
Some weblike tentacles reaching out
toward rounded rotundas.

Molded by no one.

Here
starshaped with tiny speckles,
are these the intruders in my garden
of new seedlings?
My garden carefully fed and fettered?
Of course.
I pronounced their execution
with a pinch of my fingers.

But here
among myriad friends
they flourish in weedy wilderness,
boldly gracing several acres
of untended land.
Tomorrow they shall be banished from their home.

And watered by many droplets
of human sweat
will sprout another college
where
disciplined minds finely honed
will grow
in carefully
planted rows.

No room for random weeds.

☐

LIFELINE

My tent is shrinking
I crawl about the ground floor
in
a death cycle

look up
and see
stitches of light.
I yearn to push out
my mouth
and reach
for deep breath.
I hear
the man
with the
bicycle pump
and
fumbling
fingers
not
feeling
his way in.

Don't you see
I hiss
the arrows at the top
narrow
to one
witness.
But he stood at my tomb
holding the tube like a corsage.

☐

A LIFE STORY

Many people do stick it out for a while
in dust free germ free people free room
in the hospital said the family doctor.
I opted for semi-lethal free smog and
daily treatments at the respiration center,
took up sculpting at Nishan Toor's studio,
made a dozen busts,
and drove myself to teaching English.

My creative energies included growing
a uterine tumor even
but the gynecologist said he would not
operate unless a lung man stood by
in case of malfunction of my upper parts
while he was into my lower parts.
The lung man then took more X-rays and more
tests and declared:
  Looks like
  usual asthma to me.

After seven years of being out of practice
living with the notion of not dying
took some getting used to
but then most of the time now
we can live with it.

☐

MODELS

Rows of white flags
in the rain
fluttered a livid invitation
to open houses.
Eyes unblinking watched us
march gently
into the underseas
drowned town
where blue fallopian lamps
lit the cement walls.
We arrived in hard skulls
and entered a skeletal sconce
which became our home.
Now we live here
willingly.

☐

IN SANTA CRUZ

Pliable pines
following earth's bent
leaned towards winds
past and gone.

I heard words of passersby
Look
Those trees
How natural!

Under these shades
making rhythmic
directional arrows
my young child tumbled
loped
strained against
steel supports.
Fell.

Here you go
my wind up doll
on your pins,
I said.
Metallic music.
Look Mother,
I can almost touch.

Home again
my tool snapped away
wires crippling
a Christmas gift:
my bonsai.

☐

WELFARE ISLAND

for Rose

There's our prize
patient old abbie envied by all
in ward D for her loving
sons daughters cousins
who come in
turns a clockwork parade
arms outstretched bringing
things   kisses   one-minute games.

Three mercurial grandchildren today
see how she charades for them
their little family butterfly
with no voice.
Watch now
abbie makes a sign with two fingers.

They play:
Penny's poodle had two puppies, grandma?
Sammy's cut his second tooth?
No?
No dummies
grandma's making a V, not two
Jack's team won today?
Yes, see, she nods, I'm right.

There they go
they bounce and troop out
everyday the same
different people and there abbie sits
happy and enclosed in her
metal framed bed all eyes
watch.
Now ward D will sleep
with no memories
but listen
that slow moaning
from the throat with no voice.

Abbie
are you okay?
Shall I call a doctor?

☐

SILVER ANNIVERSARY

On the surface you hardly noticed
a ripple
you never suspected that
with every stroke, so much
seaweed
would drip from your fingertips.

I have been busy
these last twenty-five years
feeding barnacles
with sharp teeth,
filling castaway bottles,
greening rocks
and covering your undersides
with chains of nippled beads
and warm moss.

If you put me out to dry
my verdant handwriting
will stretch wide across
the beach.
I will crunch beneath
you at every step
and then
when the tide turns
I will come alive in the water
like an involuted Japanese flower.

At night we work
to loosen our tangled limbs
leave trails of
phosphorescent sparks.

☐

ANOTHER MODEL

I did a reading with the women
in the Watts poetry group
and they said
We aren't into this women's lib thing
because we are still developing.
I talked with a Third World woman
at the International Women's Conference
and she said
I'm not into this women's lib thing
because I am still helping
our men
who are still developing.

I say
in my small frame
are two super developed cultures
but look
where I am!

☐

PUNCH BAG

I flaunted the spectre
of my liberation
and Yosh said
A good insurance policy
in widowhood you will do well.

☐

MIRROR MIRROR

People keep asking where I come from
says my son.
Trouble is   I'm american on the inside
        and oriental on the outside

    No Kai
    Turn that outside in
    THIS is what American looks like.

☐

Other Titles from Kitchen Table: Women of Color Press

Narratives: Poems in the Tradition of Black Women by Cheryl Clarke, $5.95 paper.

Cuentos: Stories by Latinas, Alma Gómez, Cherríe Moraga, and Mariana Romo-Carmona, eds., $9.95 paper.

Home Girls: A Black Feminist Anthology, Barbara Smith, ed., $13.95 paper, $26.95 cloth.

This Bridge Called My Back: Writings by Radical Women of Color, Cherríe Moraga and Gloria Anzaldúa, eds., $9.95 paper, $21.95 cloth.

A Comrade Is As Precious As a Rice Seedling by Mila D. Aguilar, $6.95 paper.

Desert Run, Poems and Stories by Mitsuye Yamada, $7.95 paper, $17.95 cloth.

Seventeen Syllables, and Other Stories by Hisaye Yamamoto, $9.95 paper, $21.95 cloth.

Healing Heart, poems by Gloria T. Hull, $8.95 paper, $19.95 cloth.

Freedom Organizing Series

#1 *The Combahee River Collective Statement*, Foreword by Barbara Smith, $3.50 paper.

#2 *Apartheid U.S.A.* by Audre Lorde and *Our Common Enemy, Our Common Cause: Freedom Organizing in the Eighties* by Merle Woo, $3.50 paper.

#3 *I Am Your Sister: Black Women Organizing Across Sexualities* by Audre Lorde, $3.50 paper.

#4 *It's A Family Affair: The Real Lives of Black Single Mothers* by Barbara Omolade, $3.50 paper.

#5 *Violence Against Women and the Ongoing Challenge to Racism* by Angela Y. Davis, $3.50 paper.

#6 *Need: A Chorale for Black Woman Voices* by Audre Lorde, $3.50 paper.

   African American Women in Defense of Ourselves poster commemorating the *New York Times* ad signed by 1,603 Black women in protest against the Anita Hill-Clarence Thomas Senate hearings, $15.95.

When ordering please include $1.75 postage and handling for the first book and $ .50 for each additional book. Please add $3.00 for the first poster ordered and $1.75 for each additional poster. For overseas orders please include $2.50 (U.S.) postage and handling for each book requested. Order from Kitchen Table: Women of Color Press, P.O. Box 908, Latham, NY 12110.